WITHDR

The Many Days

The Many Days

Selected Poems of Norman MacCaig

EDITED WITH AN INTRODUCTION BY

RODERICK WATSON

First published in Great Britain in 2010 by Polygon,
an imprint of Birlinn Ltd

Birlinn Ltd
West Newington House
10 Newington Road
Edinburgh
EH9 1QS

8

www.polygonbooks.co.uk

ISBN: 978 1 84697 171 6
EBOOK ISBN: 978 0 85790 780 6

The publisher acknowledges investment from Creative Scotland
towards the publication of this book.

British Library Cataloguing-in-Publication Data
A catalogue record for this book is available
on request from the British Library.

Typeset in Dante by Koinonia, Bury, Lancashire
Printed and bound in Great Britain by Clays Ltd, Elcograf S.p.A.

Contents

Likenesses

Among Scholars

Old Maps and New

From My Window

Balances

In That Other World

A Man in My Position

Introduction

'His poems are discovered in flight, migratory, wheeling and calling. Everything is in a state of restless becoming: once his attention lights on a subject, it immediately grows lambent.' In this description, Seamus Heaney gets to the heart of Norman MacCaig's verse. Time and again MacCaig brings us to a moment of evanescent delight, to a humane epiphany of love and mortality in that good place we know as the world around us, but hardly ever *see* so clearly. MacCaig's clear-sightedness is almost a matter of creative moral duty (one thinks of him as a conscientious objector during the Second World War). His imagination, in turn, allows us to see the world afresh, newly minted with surprise and delight: a goat 'with amber dumb-bells in his eyes', or that cow 'bringing its belly home, slung from a pole', or the thorn bush that traps stars in 'an encyclopaedia of angles'.

MacCaig's metaphors are well known and loved by the thousands of readers and listeners who enjoy his work. In poem after poem he leads us to make the leap that will reveal the connection, but also the disconnection, between the metaphor and the thing itself. The poet is always aware of the gap, sometimes ironically, often humorously, and sometimes – as an artist – in despair of ever really bridging it. Thus there are darker and more personal poems in this selection that speak of moments like the 'ragged man' waiting for him in the poem 'Bright day, dark centre', or the need 'to feel the world like a straitjacket' in 'On the pier at Kinlochbervie', where the strain of the poem's opening metaphor about 'a bluetit the size of the world' pecking the stars out 'one by one' speaks for a moment of personal terror by turning one of his fond and familiar creative leaps into something simultaneously 'ludicrous' and menacing.

Such dichotomies are never far from the surface in MacCaig, and yet the landscape he shows us in his work, like the peaceable kingdom of animals and people and mountains that he found in Assynt, is everywhere, finally, infused with a caring attention. Seamus Heaney sees a link with early Irish verse and the Scottish Gaelic tradition in 'the clarity of image, the sensation of blinking awake in a pristine world, the unpathetic nature of nature in his work', and MacCaig specifically invoked that tradition with the praise poems he wrote for a road, a collie, a boat, a thorn bush – humble subjects, so radiantly realised.

The collective achievement of MacCaig's lyrics is unprecedented in modern poetry. I cannot think of any other poet anywhere who has so faithfully and so persistently explored the act of noticing, and the nature of being in the world, through the thousands of epiphanic moments that are his poems, in a creative career of sixteen collections and more than fifty years. Such stern commitment to a single craft, and such generous devotion to the illumination of the world, has an almost monk-like quality to it, although MacCaig – no lover of organised religion – would have hated the comparison. But if you think of it as a secular devotion, and remember the strange little monsters to be found in the margins of the pages of the Book of Kells, then perhaps the analogy will hold.

It has not been easy to make a selection from the treasure house of the complete poems. I was helped in this task and owe a debt of thanks to Tom Pow, Alan Taylor and Ewen McCaig. Our meetings were lively as we tried to strike a balance between representing the much-loved poems that any reader would expect to find in a selected MacCaig, and choosing less familiar verses. The titled sections in this book are my way of perhaps providing new contexts for even the most well-known verses, and for allowing MacCaig's own lines to reveal common themes and preoccupations in his work. Thus each section starts with a title poem that sets the scene for the selection to follow: *Among Scholars*, for example, introduces a series of poems that revolve around MacCaig's regular sojourns in Achmelvich and the west of Scotland, while the poems in *From My Window* speak of his time in cities and most especially in Edinburgh. The section entitled *Old Maps and New* reminds us that MacCaig has often reflected – directly and indirectly – on Scottish history, not least in his long poem 'A Man In Assynt', whose personal-political focus must be included in any proper account of his work. The verses in *Likenesses* reflect – sometimes self-critically – on the poet's own penchant for metaphor and have insights to offer on the nature of the creative process itself. Under *Ineducable Me* we find poems of a more personal aspect, humorous and sometimes disturbingly painful, from a writer who had nothing but contempt and distrust for 'gush' and the so-called confessional poetry of the 1960s. The poems of *One of the Many Days* bring us to the Edenic world of creatures and landscapes that is the setting for some of Norman's most popular lyrics, just as those in *Balances* remind us that the human world has a darker side to it that no poet can escape or ignore. And if the prevailing spirit of MacCaig's achievement is still one of surprise and delight, then the reflections on death and personal loss from *In That Other World* remind us that intimations of mortality underlie the beauty of all existence, and have powered the heart of every fine lyric that has ever been written. But in the end for MacCaig, and not just for the poems that make up the final section, *A Man in My Position*, the first and the last word, clear-eyed, sardonic or tender, has always been love.

But no editorial categorisation can ever do justice to the way MacCaig's themes interpenetrate each other with surprise, humour, terror and delight at every turn of every line. Nor are these sections meant to suggest otherwise; rather they are a way of encouraging MacCaig's own poems to speak *for* themselves and (in this arrangement) *among* themselves, to set up the best kind of creative dialogue, section to section, poem to poem.

Everything speaks to everything else in MacCaig's work and, despite those wonderful frogs, he never wrote simply 'an animal poem' in his life.

Roderick Watson

Ineducable Me

Ineducable me

I don't learn much, I'm a man
of no improvements. My nose still snuffs the air
in an amateurish way. My profoundest ideas
were once toys on the floor, I love them, I've licked
most of the paint off. A whisky glass
is a rattle I don't shake. When I love
a person, a place, an object, I don't see
what there is to argue about.

I learned words, I learned words: but half of them
died for lack of exercise. And the ones I use
often look at me
with a look that whispers, *Liar*.

How I admire the eider duck that dives
with a neat loop and no splash and the gannet that suddenly
harpoons the sea. – I'm a guillemot
that still dives
in the first way it thought of: poke your head under
and fly down.

Climbing Suilven

I nod and nod to my own shadow and thrust
A mountain down and down.
Between my feet a loch shines in the brown,
Its silver paper crinkled and edged with rust.
My lungs say No;
But down and down this treadmill hill must go.

Parishes dwindle. But my parish is
This stone, that tuft, this stone
And the cramped quarters of my flesh and bone.
I claw that tall horizon down to this;
And suddenly
My shadow jumps huge miles away from me.

Sleeping compartment

I don't like this, being carried sideways
through the night. I feel wrong and helpless – like
a timber broadside in a fast stream.

Such a way of moving may suit
that odd snake the sidewinder
in Arizona: but not me in Perthshire.

I feel at rightangles to everything,
a crossgrain in existence. – It scrapes
the top of my head and my footsoles.

To forget outside is no help either –
then I become a blockage
in the long gut of the train.

I try to think I'm an Alice in Wonderland
mountaineer bivouacked
on a ledge five feet high.

It's no good. I go sidelong.
I rock sideways ... I draw in my feet
to let Aviemore pass.

Lord of Creation

At my age, I find myself
making a mountainous landscape
of the bedclothes. A movement
of knee and foot
and there's Cul Mor and a hollow
filled with Loch Sionascaig.
I watch tiny sheep stringing along
a lower slope.

Playing at God.

One day, when I go back to Assynt,
this could frighten me, this could make me
have to drive from my mind
a leg stretching out under ground, the collapse
of Cul Mor, the shedding
in every torrential direction
of Loch Sionascaig. But now
I cock up my left foot and create
Suilven. I watch myself
fishing from a rocky point.

– I think, *At my age*! – and
stretch out. My image vanishes.

God has destroyed himself again.

Private

Those who recognise my mask and recognise
my words – all to be found in the dictionary –
shall I scare them, bore them
with a truth? Shall I distort
the words to be found in the dictionary
in order to say what they mean
when they mean me?

How my friends would turn away
from the ugly sounds coming from my mouth.
How they would grieve for
that comfortable MacCaig whose
small predictions were predictable.
How they would wish back
the clean white bandages
that hid these ugly wounds.

Go away, Ariel

Heartless, musical Ariel,
does everyone prefer Caliban to you,
as I do?

Supersonic Ariel, go zip round the world
or curl up in a cowslip's bell.
I'd rather be visited by Caliban.

As I am, I am. I chat with him
helplessly spilling out of an armchair,
scaly on the carpet.

I'm teaching him to smoke. It soothes him
when he blubbers about Miranda and
goes on about his mother.

Phone a bat, Ariel. Leave us
to have a good cry – to stare at each other
with recognition and loathing.

Patriot

My only country
is six feet high
and whether I love it or not
I'll die
for its independence.

Small lochs

He's obsessed with clocks, she with politics,
He with motor cars, she with amber and jet.
There's something to be obsessed with for all of us.
Mine is lochs, the smaller the better.

I look at the big ones – Loch Ness, Loch Lomond,
Loch Shin, Loch Tay – and I bow respectfully,
But they're too grand to be invited home.
How could I treat them in the way they'd expect?

But the Dog Loch runs in eights when I go walking.
The Cat Loch purrs on the windowsill. I wade
Along Princes Street through Loch na Barrack.
In smoky bars I tell them like beads.

And don't think it's just the big ones that are lordlily named.
I met one once and when I asked what she was called
The little thing said (without blushing, mind you)
The Loch of the Corrie of the Green Waterfalls.

I know they're just H_2O in a hollow.
Yet not much time passes without me thinking of them
Dandling lilies and talking sleepily
And standing huge mountains on their watery heads.

London to Edinburgh

I'm waiting for the moment
when the train crosses the Border
and home creeps closer
at seventy miles an hour.

I dismiss the last four days
and their friendly strangers
into the past
that grows bigger every minute.

The train sounds urgent as I am,
it says home and home and home.
I light a cigarette
and sit smiling in the corner.

Scotland, I rush towards you
into my future that,
every minute,
grows smaller and smaller.

Portobello waterfront

It's acquired a French look – parasols
and bikinis and beach balls and
surf boarding and bullying speedboats.

When I was a boy, it was proletarian Scotch –
cloth caps, donkeys, Fun City,
the Salvation Army, beery faces
snoring under the Daily Record.

I'd like to make a gesture. Dare I paddle
with my trousers rolled up to the knee
and my shoes hanging round my neck?

I watch a birdwatcher. He steals
a gull from the air and imprisons it
in his binoculars, as I do
 with the year 1920.

– And I see my father
six feet two of him; St. Vitus dancing
along the cakewalk;
and into my mouth steals the taste
of sand and icecream and salty fingers.

Journeys

Travelling's fine – the stars tell me that,
and waves, and wind, and trees in the wind
tugging to go farther than their feet will let them.
Poor feet, clogged with the world.

Travelling's fine – when she's at the end of it,
or mountains breathing their vivid Esperanto,
or ideas flashing from
their always receding headlands.

There are other bad journeys, to a bitter place
I can't get to – yet. I lean towards it,
tugging to get there, and thank God
I'm clogged with the world. It grips me,
I hold it.

On a beach

There's something I want to forget,
though I forget what it is.

… My mind niggles and grits
like the sand under my feet.

I used to know things I didn't know.
Not any more. Now I don't know
even the things I know, though I think I do.

… Little waves slide up the beach and slide back,
lisping all the way. The moon
is their memory. In my head
there's no moon.

What I don't know I don't even think I know.
That was Socrates, conceited man.

I'm trying to remember
what I've remembered to forget.

Twenty yards away, a seal's head
looks at me
steadfastly
then tucks itself
under the surface, leaving
no ripple.

Bright day, dark centre

The dust silvers and a wind from the corner
brings a dream of clarinets
into the thick orchestra. There's a place
sending messages across the river of people;
and the sullen wharves of buildings
begin to smell of bales and distances.

I have a sad place that nobody enters
but a ragged man hooking the air
with skinny fingers. I sit beside him sometimes,
feeling his despair. His loneliness
infects me.

But today's a day of clarinets and silver
under the lucky horseshoe of the sky.
I leave him and go into the whirlpools of light,
through a jazz of gardens and heliograph windows.

– That house is my monkish cell, my fortress.

I put the key in the door and stop,
terrified that the ragged man
is sitting in my chair with his skinny fingers
tangled in his lap.

On the pier at Kinlochbervie

The stars go out one by one
as though a bluetit the size of the world
were pecking them like peanuts out of the sky's string bag,

A ludicrous image, I know.

Take away the gray light.
I want the bronze shields of summer
or winter's scalding sleet.

My mind is struggling with itself.

That fishing boat is a secret
approaching me. It's a secret
coming out of another one.
I want to know the first one of all.

Everything's in the distance,
as I am. I wish I could flip that distance
like a cigarette into the water.

I want an extreme of nearness.
I want boundaries on my mind.
I want to feel the world like a straitjacket.

Emblems: after her illness

They went away, the sad times.
It wasn't I who turned them out of doors,
but another.

The swifts have returned. They've dropped
their burden of long journeys. With what joy
they scream over the rooftops.

Pour the coffee. Sit by the fire
that says *home*. Tomorrow we'll welcome
all the tomorrows there are to be.

Do you hear the swifts? They tie together
the bright light. They nest
in secret places.

Sargasso Sea

Tangled in weeds.
Far from home.
On an ocean
I've nothing to do with.

How I envy the elvers
who leave their Sargasso and drift
across the Atlantic.

So many will find
the river I know best.
How eagerly they swim
against its rushing torrent

that brings them news
from high places
I once visited
long ago.

By the Three Lochans

I sit, trying to look like a heather bush –
hoping to see
a mewing buzzard or a vole or a dragonfly.
How quickly the days slide away
into where they came from.

It's hard to change anything.
I look into my hand to see
if there's an idea there
giving birth to a strenuous baby.
Only a life-line that's not long enough.

An obstinate old rowan tree
stands on a tiny island.
So many storms, yet there it is
with only a few berries, each determined
to be the last one to drop into the water.

And the light floods down
revealing mountains and flowers
and so many shadows. If only
a merlin would hurtle past, that atom
of speed, that molecule of life.

Hugh MacDiarmid

When he speaks a small sentence
he is a man
who presses a plunger that will
blow the face off a cliff.

Or: one last small penstroke –
and the huge poem rides
down the slipway, ready
for enormous voyages.

He does more than he does.
When he goes hunting
he aims at a bird and
brings a landscape down.

Or he dynamites a ramshackle
idea – when
the dust settles,
what structures shine in the sun.

After his death

for Hugh MacDiarmid

It turned out
that the bombs he had thrown
raised buildings:

that the acid he had sprayed
had painfully opened
the eyes of the blind.

Fishermen hauled
prizewinning fish
from the water he had polluted.

We sat with astonishment
enjoying the shade
of the vicious words he had planted.

The government decreed that
on the anniversary of his birth
the people should observe
two minutes pandemonium.

Grand-daughter visiting

She balances things – a brick upon a brick:
a ring in one hand, a spoon in the other:
and the two nine months she's lived.

Her home is warmed by the steady
glow of electric fires; but here
she holds a brick over another brick
to stare at the flames jumping
in the grate. With what concentration
she stares at them.

Soon she'll unbalance
that first nine months with nine years,
with nineteen years: her left hand won't know
what her right hand is doing; and who can guess
what fires she will stare at,
sitting in a scatter of forgotten toys?

To be a leaf

My 3 year old, after being a seal
and a daffodil and a frog
demanded – Glampa!
Be a leaf!

To hang nicely on a twig tip or snug
in a bosomly branch, to rockabye, to entertain
a star or two …

A caterpillar loops in my mind, a goat snatches,
the wintry earth
draws my blood from me.

And the tree of my veins
is an aspen trembling.

I hold her, pulling out
the softest of thorns.

Between mountain and sea

Honey and salt – land smell and sea smell,
as in the long ago, as in forever.

The days pick me up and carry me off,
half-child, half-prisoner,

on their journey that I'll share
for a while.

They wound and they bless me
with strange gifts:

the salt of absence,
the honey of memory.

One of the Many Days

One of the many days

I never saw more frogs
than once at the back of Ben Dorain.
Joseph-coated, they ambled and jumped
in the sweet marsh grass
like coloured ideas.

The river ran glass in the sun.
I waded in the jocular water
of Loch Lyon. A parcel of hinds
gave the V-sign with their ears, then
ran off and off till they were
cantering crumbs. I watched
a whole long day
release its miracles.

But clearest of all I remember
the Joseph-coated frogs
amiably ambling or
jumping into the air – like
coloured ideas
tinily considering
the huge concept of Ben Dorain.

Feeding ducks

One duck stood on my toes.
The others made watery rushes after bread
Thrown by my momentary hand; instead,
She stood duck-still and got far more than those.
An invisible drone boomed by
With a beetle in it; the neighbour's yearning bull
Bugled across five fields. And an evening full
Of other evenings quietly began to die.

And my everlasting hand
Dropped on my hypocrite duck her grace of bread.
And I thought, 'The first to be fattened, the first to be dead',
Till my gestures enlarged, wide over the darkening land.

Goat

The goat, with amber dumb-bells in his eyes,
The blasé lecher, inquisitive as sin,
White sarcasm walking, proof against surprise,

The nothing like him goat, goat-in-itself,
Idea of goatishness made flesh, pure essence
In idle masquerade on a rocky shelf –

Hangs upside down from lushest grass to twitch
A shrivelled blade from the cliff's barren chest,
And holds the grass well lost; the narrowest niche

Is frame for the devil's face; the steepest thatch
Of barn or byre is pavement to his foot;
The last, loved rose a prisoner to his snatch;

And the man in his man-ness, passing, feels suddenly
Hypocrite found out, hearing behind him that
Vulgar vibrato, thin derisive me-eh.

Byre

The thatched roof rings like heaven where mice
Squeak small hosannahs all night long,
Scratching its golden pavements, skirting
The gutter's crystal river-song.

Wild kittens in the world below
Glare with one flaming eye through cracks,
Spurt in the straw, are tawny brooches
Splayed on the chests of drunken sacks.

The dimness becomes darkness as
Vast presences come mincing in,
Swagbellied Aphrodites, swinging
A silver slaver from each chin.

And all is milky, secret, female.
Angels are hushed and plain straws shine.
And kittens miaow in circles, stalking
With tail and hindleg one straight line.

Fetching cows

The black one, last as usual, swings her head
And coils a black tongue round a grass-tuft. I
Watch her soft weight come down, her split feet spread.

In front, the others swing and slouch; they roll
Their great Greek eyes and breathe out milky gusts
From muzzles black and shiny as wet coal.

The collie trots, bored, at my heels, then plops
Into the ditch. The sea makes a tired sound
That's always stopping though it never stops.

A haycart squats prickeared against the sky.
Hay breath and milk breath. Far out in the West
The wrecked sun founders though its colours fly.

The collie's bored. There's nothing to control …
The black cow is two native carriers
Bringing its belly home, slung from a pole.

Blind horse

He snuffles towards
pouches of water in the grass
and doesn't drink
when he finds them.

He twitches listlessly
at sappy grass stems and stands
stone still, his hanging head
caricatured with a scribble
of green whiskers.

Sometimes that head swings high,
ears cock – and he stares
down a long sound,
he stares and whinnies
for what never comes.

His eyes never close,
not in the heat of the day
when his leather lip droops and
he wears blinkers of flies.

At any time of the night
you hear him in his dark field
stamp the ground, stamp
the world down, waiting impatiently
for the light to break.

Frogs

Frogs sit more solid
than anything sits. In mid-leap they are
parachutists falling
in a free fall. They die on roads
with arms across their chests and
heads high.

I love frogs that sit
like Buddha, that fall without
parachutes, that die
like Italian tenors.

Above all, I love them because,
pursued in water, they never
panic so much that they fail
to make stylish triangles
with their ballet dancer's
legs.

Basking shark

To stub an oar on a rock where none should be,
To have it rise with a slounge out of the sea
Is a thing that happened once (too often) to me.

But not too often – though enough. I count as gain
That once I met, on a sea tin-tacked with rain,
That roomsized monster with a matchbox brain.

He displaced more than water. He shoggled me
Centuries back – this decadent townee
Shook on a wrong branch of his family tree.

Swish up the dirt and, when it settles, a spring
Is all the clearer. I saw me, in one fling,
Emerging from the slime of everything.

So who's the monster? The thought made me grow pale
For twenty seconds while, sail after sail,
The tall fin slid away and then the tail.

Wild oats

Every day I see from my window
pigeons, up on a roof ledge – the males
are wobbling gyroscopes of lust.

Last week a stranger joined them, a snowwhite
pouting fantail,
Mae West in the Women's Guild.
What becks, what croo-croos, what
demented pirouetting, what a lack
of moustaches to stroke.

The females – no need to be one of them
to know
exactly what they were thinking – pretended

she wasn't there
and went dowdily on with whatever
pigeons do when they're knitting.

Sparrow

He's no artist.
His taste in clothes is more
dowdy than gaudy.
And his nest – that blackbird, writing
pretty scrolls on the air with the gold nib of his beak,
would call it a slum.

To stalk solitary on lawns,
to sing solitary in midnight trees,
to glide solitary over gray Atlantics –
not for him: he'd rather
a punch-up in a gutter.

He carries what learning he has
lightly – it is, in fact, based only
on the usefulness whose result
is survival. A proletarian bird.
No scholar.
But when winter soft-shoes in
and these other birds –
ballet dancers, musicians, architects –
die in the snow
and freeze to branches,
watch him happily flying
on the O-levels and A-levels
of the air.

Blackbird in a sunset bush

Everything's in the sunset. Windows
flare in it, rooms blush.
Cars scatter everywhere – they make the city
one huge pintable. Life is opulent
as thunder.

Only the blackbird there
contemplates
what the sunset's in:
what makes a flower ponderous
and breathes a mountain away.

The gravity of beauty –
how thoughtfully, how pensively he puts it,
charcoal philosopher
in his blazing study.

Ringed plover by a water's edge

They sprint eight feet and –
stop. Like that. They
sprintayard (like that) and
stop.
They have no acceleration
and no brakes.
Top speed's their only one.

They're alive – put life
through a burning-glass, they're
its focus – but they share
the world of delicate clockwork.

In spasmodic
Indian file
they parallel the parallel ripples.

When they stop
they, suddenly,
are gravel.

Dipper

No webbed feet,
but a water bird for all that.

And a gentlemanly one –
he walks on the bottom
of his helter-skelter stream
wearing a white shirt front
and a brown cummerbund.

He hates dry land.
Flying up a twisty stream
he follows the twists
all the way.
When he perches on a stone
it's a wet one.
He stands there, bobbing and bobbing
as though the water's applauding him.

He likes his nest
to be behind a rippling tapestry –
a tapestry? Well,
a waterfall.

Naturally.

Toad

Stop looking like a purse. How could a purse
squeeze under the rickety door and sit,
full of satisfaction, in a man's house?

You clamber towards me on your four corners –
right hand, left foot, left hand, right foot.

I love you for being a toad,
for crawling like a Japanese wrestler,
and for not being frightened.

I put you in my purse hand, not shutting it,
and set you down outside directly under
every star.

A jewel in your head? Toad,
you've put one in mine,
a tiny radiance in a dark place.

Blue tit on a string of peanuts

A cubic inch of some stars
weighs a hundred tons – Blue tit,
who could measure the power
of your tiny spark of energy? Your hair-thin legs
(one north-east, one due west) support
a scrap of volcano, four inches
of hurricane: and, seeing me, you make the sound
of a grain of sawdust being sawn
by the minutest of saws.

My last word on frogs

People have said to me, *You seem to like frogs.*
They keep jumping into your poems.

I do. I love the way they sit,
compact as a cat and as indifferent
to everything but style, like a lady remembering
to keep her knees together. And I love
the elegant way they jump and
the inelegant way they land.
So human.

I feel so close to them
I must be froggish myself.
I look in the mirror expecting to see
a fairytale Prince.

But no. It's just sprawling me,
croaking away
and swivelling my eyes around
for the stealthy heron and his stabbing beak.

Our neighbour's cat

Night is in the garden.
In both the black cat
is a small black sculpture
in the long grass.

I watch for ten minutes.
She never moves.

A plane flies high
over the city. She looks up.
Her eyes steal the moon.

I'm tired. I go to bed
and stretch out in it.

Sculpturesque, I think,
as my eyes
steal the darkness.

Gin trap

In the wide bogland a hoodie crow,
six feet from the trap that had maimed him,
tries to stand, tries to fly.

In the rags of his feathers, with mad eyes,
he surges about in the heather. Sometimes
his frantic voice adds its ugliness
to the terror and the pain.

Little Lear, you have no Cordelia
to lament for, no steepdown gulfs
of liquid fire to burn you away
into a cindery darkness.

Your friends will come, your hoodie companions,
with their dreadful requiems – or
a gliding fox will tear you apart
with his flashing, beautiful smile.

Likenesses

Likenesses

It comes to mind,
Where there is room enough, that water goes
Between tall mountains and between small toes.

Or, if I like,
When the sun rises, his first light explores
Under high clouds and underneath low doors.

Or (doing it still)
Darkness can hide beside all that it hid
Behind a nightfall and a dropped eyelid.

Why do I add
Such notions up, unless they say what's true
In ways I don't quite see, of me and you?

Instrument and agent

In my eye I've no apple; every object
Enters in there with hands in pockets.
I welcome them all, just as they are,
Every one equal, none a stranger.

Yet in the short journey they make
To my skull's back, each takes a look
From another, or a gesture, or
A special way of saying *Sir*.

So tree is partly girl; moon
And wit slide through the sky together;
And which is star – what's come a million
Miles or gone those inches farther?

Summer farm

Straws like tame lightnings lie about the grass
And hang zigzag on hedges. Green as glass
The water in the horse-trough shines.
Nine ducks go wobbling by in two straight lines.

A hen stares at nothing with one eye,
Then picks it up. Out of an empty sky
A swallow falls and, flickering through
The barn, dives up again into the dizzy blue.

I lie, not thinking, in the cool, soft grass,
Afraid of where a thought might take me – as
This grasshopper with plated face
Unfolds his legs and finds himself in space.

Self under self, a pile of selves I stand
Threaded on time, and with metaphysic hand
Lift the farm like a lid and see
Farm within farm, and in the centre, me.

Linguist

If we lived in a world where bells
truly say 'ding-dong' and where 'moo'
is a rather neat thing
said by a cow,
I could believe you could believe
that these sounds I make in the air
and these shapes with which I blacken white paper
have some reference
to the thoughts in my mind
and the feelings in the thoughts.

As things are
if I were to gaze in your eyes and say
'bow-wow' or 'quack', you must take that to be

a despairing anthology of praises,
a concentration of all the opposites
of reticence, a capsule
of my meaning of meaning
that I can no more write down
than I could spell the sound of the sigh
I would then utter, before
dingdonging and mooing my way
through all the lexicons and languages
of imprecision.

Leaving the Museum of Modern Art

I went out from the unsheltered world of art
into the unsheltered world,
and there, by the door –
Picasso's Goat –
a shape of iron entered into by herds,
by every aspect of goatishness.
(What are you to say of a man
who can carve a smell, who
can make a goat-smell out of iron?)

This is the lie of art
telling its great truth:
a shape of iron, destructible and
created, being a revelation about life,
that is destructive and
indestructible.

From now on,
whatever of life passes
my understanding, I know more of it
than I did, being
a professor of goats, a pedant
of goatishness.

Painting – 'The Blue Jar'

The blue jar jumps forward
thrust into the room
by the colours round about it.

I wonder,
since it's thrust forward,
what true thing lies
in the fictitious space
behind it.

I sink into my surroundings,
leaving in front of me a fictitious space
where I can be invented.

But the blue jar helplessly
presents itself. It holds out a truth
on a fiction. It keeps its place
by being out of it.

I admire the muscles of pigments
that can hold out a jar for years
without trembling.

Helpless collector

Events come
bringing me presents –
more, as has been said, than the sands of the sea,
more, as has been said oftener, than the stars in the sky.

There's no refusal.

I'm the lucky possessor
of the ones that please me. I try to be
only the caretaker
of the ones I hate.

They won't let me.

I put the crooked mask
behind the delicate jar
and it moves to the front.

No choice

I think about you
in as many ways as rain comes.

(I am growing, as I get older,
to hate metaphors – their exactness
and their inadequacy.)

Sometimes these thoughts are
a moistness, hardly falling, than which
nothing is more gentle:
sometimes, a rattling shower, a
bustling Spring-cleaning of the mind:
sometimes, a drowning downpour.

I am growing, as I get older,
to hate metaphor,
to love gentleness,
to fear downpours.

Recipe

You have to be stubborn.
You have to turn away
from meditation, from ideologies,
from the tombstone face
of the Royal Bank of Scotland.

You have to keep stubbornly saying
This is bread, though it's in a sunset,
this is a sunset with bread in it.
This is a woman, she doesn't live
in a book or an imagination.
Hello, water, you must say, *Hello, good water.*

You have to touch wood, but not for luck.
You have to listen to that matter of pitches and crescendos
without thinking Beethoven is speaking
only to you.

And you must learn there are words
with no meaning, words like *consolation*,
words like *goodbye*.

Also

You try to help, and what happens?
You hurt also.

You hoist a sail on a boat
and one day, gusted sideways,
the boat is scattered in timbers
round a slavering rock.
You put violets in water, and what happens?
They lose all their scent.

And you give absence and loneliness and fear
when you give love – that full sail,
that sweet water.

No end to them

I said, Never again will I write
about love, or frogs, or absence
or the heart-stopping intrusion
of steep-down, steep-up mountains.

Satisfied, I sat down and was overwhelmed
with sheet lightnings of revelations
of new things, of absolutely new things.

Twitching with joy, I scribbled for days
– about what?

About love and frogs and absence …
etcetera.

Oh, William Blake and your grain of sand,
what a consolation you are to me.
I'll scuttle happily in my matchbox labyrinth
seeking no way out,
meeting my small marvels round every corner
till I meet the last one
swaying his heavy horns
in that shadowy dead end.

Landscape and I

Landscape and I get on together well.
Though I'm the talkative one, still he can tell
His symptoms of being to me, the way a shell
Murmurs of oceans.

Loch Rannoch lapses dimpling in the sun.
Its hieroglyphs of light fade one by one
But re-create themselves, their message done,
For ever and ever.

That sprinkling lark jerked upward in the blue
Will daze to nowhere but leave himself in true
Translation – hear his song cascading through
His disappearance.

The hawk knows all about it, shaking there
An empty glove on steep chutes of the air
Till his yellow foot cramps on a squeal, to tear
Smooth fur, smooth feather.

This means, of course, Schiehallion in my mind
Is more than mountain. In it he leaves behind
A meaning, an idea, like a hind
Couched in a corrie.

So then I'll woo the mountain till I know
The meaning of the meaning, no less. Oh,
There's a Schiehallion anywhere you go.
The thing is, climb it.

Among Scholars

Among scholars

On our way to a loch, two miles from Inveruplan,
Three of us (keepers) read the landscape as
I read a book. They missed no word of it:
Fox-hole, strange weed, blue berry, ice-scrape, deer's hoof-print.
It was their back yard, and fresh as the garden in Eden
(Striped rock 'like a Belted Galloway'). They saw what I
Saw, and more, and its meaning. They spoke like a native
The language they walked in. I envied them, naturally.

Coming back, we dragged the boat down to Inveruplan,
Lurching and slithering, both it and us. A stag
Paused in the thickening light to see that strange thing,
A twelve-legged boat in a bog. Angie roared at it
Like a stag in rut. Denying its other senses
It came and paused and came – and took itself off,
A text, a chapter and verse, into its gospel.
We took up the rope and hauled on, sweating and gasping.

We left the boat in the hayfield at Inveruplan:
The tractor would get it. A moon was coming up
Over the roof and under it a Tilley lamp
Hissed in its yellow self. We took our noise
Into the room and shut it in with us
Where, till light broke on a boat foundered in dew,
I drank down drams in a company of scholars
With exploding songs and a three-days ache in my shoulder.

Midnight, Lochinver

Wine-coloured, Homer said, wine-dark …
The seaweed on the stony beach,
Flushed darker with that wine, was kilts
And beasts and carpets … A startled heron
Tucked in its cloud two yellow stilts.

And eiderducks were five, no, two –
No, six. A lounging fishbox raised
Its broad nose to the moon. With groans
And shouts the steep burn drowned itself;
And sighs were soft among the stones.

All quiet, all dark: excepting where
A cone of light stood on the pier
And in the circle of its scope
A hot winch huffed and puffed and gnashed
Its iron fangs and swallowed rope.

The nursing tide moved gently in.
Familiar archipelagos
Heard her advancing, heard her speak
Things clear, though hard to understand
Whether in Gaelic or in Greek.

Crofter's kitchen, evening

A man's boots with a woman in them
Clatter across the floor. A hand
Long careless of the lives it kills
Comes down and thwacks on newspapers
A long black fish with bloody gills.

The kettle's at her singsong – minor
Prophetess in her sooty cave.
A kitten climbs the bundled net
On the bench and, curled up like a cowpat,
Purrs on the *Stornoway Gazette*.

The six hooks of a Mackerel Dandy
Climb their thin rope – an exclamation
By the curled question of a gaff.
Three rubber eels cling like a crayfish
On top of an old photograph.

Peats fur themselves in gray. The door
Bursts open, chairs creak, a hand reaches out
For spectacles, a lamp flares high …
The collie underneath the table
Slumps with a world-rejecting sigh.

By Achmelvich bridge

Night stirs the trees
With breathings of such music that they sway,
Skirts, sleeves, tiaras, in the humming dark,
Their highborn heads tossing in disarray.

A floating owl
Unreels his silence, winding in and out
Of different darknesses. The wind takes up
And scatters a sound of water all about.

No moon need slide
Into the sky to make that water bright;
It ties its swelling self with glassy ropes;
It jumps from stones in smithereens of light.

The mosses on the wall
Plump their fat cushions up. They smell of wells,
Of under bridges and of spoons. They move
More quiveringly than the dazed rims of bells.

A broad cloud drops
A darker darkness. Turning up his stare,
Letting the world pour under him, owl goes off,
His small soft foghorn quavering through the air.

Neglected graveyard, Luskentyre

I wade in the long grass,
Barking my shins on gravestones.
The grass overtops the dyke.
In and out of the bay hesitates the Atlantic.

A seagull stares at me hard
With a quarterdeck eye, leans forward
And shrugs into the air.
The dead rest from their journey from one wilderness to another.

Considering what they were,
This seems a proper disorder.
Why lay graves by rule
Like bars of a cage on the ground? To discipline the unruly?

I know a man who is
Peeped at by death. No place is
Atlantics coming in;
No time but reaches out to touch him with a cold finger.

He hears death at the door.
He knows him round every corner.
No matter where he goes
He wades in long grass, barking his shins on gravestones.

The edge of the green sea
Crumples. Bees are in clover.
I part the grasses and there –
Angus MacLeod, drowned. Mary his wife. Together.

Moment musical in Assynt

A mountain is a sort of music: theme
And counter theme displaced in air amongst
Their own variations.
Wagnerian Devil signed the Coigach score;
And God was Mozart when he wrote Cul Mor.

You climb a trio when you climb Cul Beag.
Stac Polly – there's a rondo in seven sharps,
Neat as a trivet.
And Quinag, rallentando in the haze,
Is one long tune extending phrase by phrase.

I listen with my eyes and see through that
Mellifluous din of shapes my masterpiece
Of masterpieces:
One sandstone chord that holds up time in space –

Sforzando Suilven reared on his ground bass.

Two shepherds

Donald roared and ran and brandished
his stick and swore
in all the languages
he knew, which were
some.

Pollóchan sauntered, stood
six feet three silent: with a small
turn of the hand
he'd send the collie flowing
round the half-mile-long arc
of a towsy circle.

Two poets –
Dionysian,
Apollonian
and the sheep in the pen.

Aunt Julia

Aunt Julia spoke Gaelic
very loud and very fast.
I could not answer her –
I could not understand her.

She wore men's boots
when she wore any.
– I can see her strong foot,
stained with peat,
paddling with the treadle of the spinningwheel
while her right hand drew yarn
marvellously out of the air.

Hers was the only house
where I've lain at night
in the absolute darkness
of a box bed, listening to
crickets being friendly.

She was buckets
and water flouncing into them.
She was winds pouring wetly
round house-ends.
She was brown eggs, black skirts
and a keeper of threepennybits
in a teapot.

Aunt Julia spoke Gaelic
very loud and very fast.
By the time I had learned
a little, she lay
silenced in the absolute black
of a sandy grave
at Luskentyre. But I hear her still, welcoming me
with a seagull's voice
across a hundred yards
of peatscrapes and lazybeds
and getting angry, getting angry
with so many questions
unanswered.

Uncle Roderick

His drifter swung in the night
from a mile of nets
between the Shiants and Harris.

My boy's eyes watched
the lights of the fishing fleet – fireflies
on the green field of the sea.

In the foc'sle he gave me a bowl
of tea, black, strong and bitter,
and a biscuit you hammered
in bits like a plate.

The fiery curtain came up
from the blackness, comma'd with corpses.

Round Rhu nan Cuideagan
he steered for home, a boy's god
in seaboots. He found his anchorage
as a bird its nest.

In the kitchen he dropped
his oilskins where he stood.

He was strong as the red bull.
He moved like a dancer.
He was a cran of songs.

The Red Well, Harris

The Red Well has gone.
Thirty years ago I filled pails from it
with a flashing dipper and floated
a frond of bracken in each
so that no splash of water should escape
from its jolting prison.

Where that eye of water once
blinked from the ground
now stands a gray house
filled with voices.

The house is solid. But
nothing will keep the children
in its happy prison
from scattering abroad, till
the house at last stands empty –
one drained well
on top of another.

Country dance

The room whirled and coloured
and figured itself with dancers.
Another gaiety seemed born of theirs
and flew as streamers
between their heads and the ceiling.

I gazed, coloured and figured,
down the tunnel of streamers –
and there, in the band, an old fiddler
sawing away in the privacy
of music. He bowed lefthanded and his right hand
was the wrong way round. Impossible.
But the jig bounced, the gracenotes
sparkled on the surface of the tune.
The odd man out, when it came to music,
was the odd man in.

There's a lesson here, I thought, climbing
into the pulpit I keep in my mind.
But before I'd said *Firstly brethren*, the tune
ended, the dancers parted, the old fiddler
took a cigarette from the pianist, stripped off
the paper and chewed the tobacco.

Return to Scalpay

The ferry wades across the kyle. I drive
The car ashore
On to a trim tarred road. A car on Scalpay?
Yes, and a road where never was one before.
The ferrymen's Gaelic wonders who I am
(Not knowing I know it), this man back from the dead,
Who takes the blue-black road (no traffic jam)
From by Craig Lexie over to Bay Head.

A man bows in the North wind, shaping up
His lazybeds,
And through the salt air vagrant peat smells waver
From houses where no house should be. The sheds
At the curing station have been newly tarred.
Aunt Julia's house has vanished. The Red Well
Has been bulldozed away. But sharp and hard
The church still stands, barring the road to Hell.

A chugging prawn boat slides round Cuddy Point
Where in a gale
I spread my batwing jacket and jumped farther
Than I've jumped since. There's where I used to sail
Boats looped from rushes. On the jetty there
I caught eels, cut their heads off and watched them slew
Slow through the water. Ah – Cape Finisterre
I called that point, to show how much I knew.

While Hamish sketches, a crofter tells me that
The Scalpay folk,
Though very intelligent, are not Spinozas …
We walk the Out End road (no need to invoke
That troublemaker, Memory, she's everywhere)
To Laggandoan, greeted all the way –
My city eyeballs prickle; it's hard to bear
With such affection and such gaiety.

Scalpay revisited? – more than Scalpay. I
Have no defence,

For half my thought and half my blood is Scalpay,
Against that pure, hardheaded innocence
That shows love without shame, weeps without shame,
Whose every thought is hospitality –
Edinburgh, Edinburgh, you're dark years away.

Scuttering snowflakes riddling the hard wind
Are almost spent
When we reach Johann's house. She fills the doorway,
Sixty years of size and astonishment,
Then laughs and cries and laughs, as she always did
And will (Easy glum, easy glow, a friend would say) …
Scones, oatcakes, herrings from under a bubbling lid.
Then she comes with us to put us on our way.

Hugging my arm in her stronger one, she says,
Fancy me
Walking this road beside my darling Norman!
And what is there to say? … We look back and see
Her monumental against the flying sky
And I am filled with love and praise and shame
Knowing that I have been, and knowing why,
Diminished and enlarged. Are they the same?

Praise of a road

You won't let me forget you. You keep nudging me
With your hairpin bends or, without a *Next, please,*
Magic-lanterning another prodigious view
In my skull where I sit in the dark with my brains.

You turn up your nose above Loch Hope,
That effete low-lier where men sit comfy
In boats, casting for seatrout, and whisper
Up the hill, round the crag – there are the Crocachs.

You're an acrobat with a bulrushy spine,
Looping in air, turning to look at yourself
And faultlessly skidding on your own stones
Round improbable corners and arriving safe.

When the Crocachs have given me mist and trout
And clogs of peat, how I greet you and whirl
Down your half-scree zigzags, tumbling like a peewit
Through trembling evenings down to Loch Eriboll.

Praise of a collie

She was a small dog, neat and fluid –
Even her conversation was tiny:
She greeted you with *bow*, never *bow-wow*.

Her sons stood monumentally over her
But did what she told them. Each grew grizzled
Till it seemed he was his own mother's grandfather.

Once, gathering sheep on a showery day,
I remarked how dry she was. Pollóchan said, 'Ah,
It would take a very accurate drop to hit Lassie.'

She sailed in the dinghy like a proper sea-dog.
Where's a burn? – she's first on the other side.
She flowed through fences like a piece of black wind.

But suddenly she was old and sick and crippled …
I grieved for Pollóchan when he took her a stroll
And put his gun to the back of her head.

Praise of a boat

The *Bateau Ivre* and the *Marie Celeste*,
The *Flying Dutchman* hurdling latitudes –
You could make a list (sad ones like the *Lusitania*
And brave puffed-up ones like the *Mayflower*).

Mine's called *the boat*. It's a quiet, anonymous one
That needs my two arms to drag it through the water.
It takes me huge distances of a few miles
From its lair in Loch Roe to fishy Soya.

It prances on the spot in its watery stable.
It butts the running tide with a bull's head.
It skims downwind, planing like a shearwater.
In crossrips it's awkward as a piano.

And what a coffin it is for haddocks
And bomb-shaped lythe and tigerish mackerel –
Though it once met a basking shark with a bump
And sailed for a while looking over its shoulder.

When salmon are about it goes glib in the dark,
Whispering a net out over the sternsheets –
How it crabs the tide-rush, the cunning thing,
While arms plunge down for the wrestling silver.

Boat of no dreams, you open spaces
The mind can't think of till it's in them,
Where the world is easy and dangerous and
Who can distinguish saints and sinners?

Sometimes that space reaches out
Till I'm enclosed in it in stony Edinburgh
And I hear you like a barrel thumping on head waves
Or in still water gurgling like a baby.

Praise of a thorn bush

You've taken your stand
between Christy MacLeod's house
and the farthest planet.

The ideal shape of a circle
means nothing to you: you're all
armpits and elbows
and scraggy fingers that hold so delicately
a few lucid roses. You are
an encyclopedia of angles.

At night you trap stars, and the moon
fills you with distances.
I arrange myself to put
one rose in the belt of Orion.

When the salt gales drag through you
you whip them with flowers
and I think –
Exclamations for you, little rose bush,
and a couple of fanfares.

Fishermen's pub

I leaned on the bar, not thinking, just noticing.
I read the labels thumbed on the bright bottles.
(To gallop on White Horse through Islay Mist!

To sail into Talisker on Windjammer Rum!)
Above my head the sick TV trembled
And by the dartboard a guitar was thrumming

Some out of place tune … Others have done this
Before me. Remember, in one of the Russias,
Alexander Blok drunk beyond his own mercy –

How he saw, through the smoke and the uproar,
His 'silken lady' come in and fire
The fire within him? I found myself staring

For mine, for that wild, miraculous presence
That would startle the world new with her forgivingness.
But nothing was there but sidling smokewreaths

And through the babble all I heard was,
(Sounding, too near, in my dreadful silence)
A foreign guitar, the death clack of dominoes.

Off Coigeach Point

Flat sea, thin mist
and a seal singing.
– And the world's an old man in his corner
telling a folktale.

Haddock goggle up, are
swung aboard. Gray as the sea mist.
They drown in air.

In the fishbox they
have nothing to do with death. They've become
a fine-line drawing
in the art gallery
of the world.

We make for home.

Near Soya
Seven seals oilily slide off a skerry
into the silky gray. Norman tells me
if he puts the engine into reverse
they turn
a back somersault.

And he does.
And they do.

Old Highland woman

She sits all day by the fire.
How long is it since she opened the door
and stepped outside, confusing
the scuffling hens and the collie
dreaming of sheep?
Her walking days are over.

She has come here through centuries
of Gaelic labour and loves
and rainy funerals. Her people

are assembled in her bones.
She's their summation. *Before her time*
has almost no meaning.

When neighbours call
she laughs a wicked cackle
with love in it, as she listens
to the sly bristle of gossip,
relishing the life in it,
relishing the malice, with her hands
lying in her lap like holy psalms
that once had a meaning for her, that once
were noble with tunes
she used to sing long ago.

Two men at once

In the Culag Bar a fiddler is playing
fast-rippling tunes with easy dexterity.

How do I know? I'm in Edinburgh

On the pier, sun-scorched tourists
hang their bellies over improbable shorts.

How do I know? I'm in Edinburgh.

In the Veyatie burn a man
hooks a trout. It starts rampaging.

And I'm in Edinburgh.

Or so I say. How easy to be
two men at once.

One smiling and drinking coffee
in Leamington Terrace, Edinburgh.

The other cutting the pack of memories
and turning up ace after ace after ace.

Old Maps and New

Old maps and new

There are spaces
where infringements are possible.
There are notices that say:
Trespassers will be welcome.

Pity leaks through the roof
of the Labour Exchange.
In the Leader's pocket,
wrapped in the plans for the great offensive,
are sweets for the children
and a crumpled letter.

There are spaces still to be filled
before the map is completed –
though these days it's only
in the explored territories
that men write, sadly,
Here live monsters.

High Street, Edinburgh

Here's where to make a winter fire of stories
And burn dead heroes to keep your shinbones warm,
Bracing the door against the jackboot storm
With an old king or two, stuffing the glories
Of rancid martyrs with their flesh on fire
Into the broken pane that looks beyond Fife
Where Alexander died and a vain desire,
Hatched in Macbeth, sat whittling at his life.

Across this gulf where skeins of duck once clattered
Round the black Rock and now a tall ghost wails
Over a shuddering train, how many tales
Have come from the hungry North of armies shattered,
An ill cause won, a useless battle lost,
A head rolled like an apple on the ground;
And Spanish warships staggering west and tossed
On frothing skerries; and a king come to be crowned.

Look out into this brown November night
That smells of herrings from the Forth and frost;
The voices humming in the air have crossed
More than the Grampians; East and West unite,
In dragonish swirlings over the city park,
Their tales of deaths and treacheries, and where
A tall dissolving ghost shrieks in the dark
Old history greets you with a Bedlam stare.

He talks more tongues than English now. He fetches
The unimagined corners of the world
To ride this smoky sky, and in the curled
Autumnal fog his phantoms move. He stretches
His frozen arm across three continents
To blur this window. Look out from it. Look out
From your November. Tombs and monuments
Pile in the air and invisible armies shout.

Celtic cross

The implicated generations made
This symbol of their lives, a stone made light
By what is carved on it.
                              The plaiting masks,
But not with involutions of a shade,
What a stone says and what a stone cross asks.

Something that is not mirrored by nor trapped
In webs of water or bag-nets of cloud;
The tangled mesh of weed
                              lets it go by.
Only men's minds could ever have unmapped
Into abstraction such a territory.

No green bay going yellow over sand
Is written on by winds to tell a tale
Of death-dishevelled gull
                              or heron, stiff
As a cruel clerk with gaunt writs in his hand
– Or even of light, that makes its depths a cliff.

Singing responses order otherwise.
The tangled generations ravelled out
In links of song whose sweet
                              strong choruses
Are these stone involutions to the eyes
Given to the ear in abstract vocables.

The stone remains, and the cross, to let us know
Their unjust, hard demands, as symbols do.
But on them twine and grow
                              beneath the dove
Serpents of wisdom whose cool statements show
Such understanding that it seems like love.

Crossing the Border

I sit with my back to the engine, watching
the landscape pouring away out of my eyes.
I think I know where I'm going and have
some choice in the matter.

I think, too, that this was a country
of bog-trotters, moss-troopers,
fired ricks and roof-trees in the black night – glinting
on tossed horns and red blades.
I think of lives
bubbling into the harsh grass.

What difference now?
I sit with my back to the future, watching
time pouring away into the past. I sit, being helplessly
lugged backwards
through the Debatable Lands of history, listening
to the execrations, the scattered cries, the
falling of roof-trees
in the lamentable dark.

Two thieves

At the Place for Pulling up Boats
(one word in Gaelic) the tide is full.
It seeps over the grass, stealthy as a robber.
Which it is.

– For old Flora tells me
that fifty yards stretch of gravel, now under water,
was, in her granny's time, a smooth green sward
where the Duke of Sutherland
turned his coach and four.

What an image of richness, a tiny pageantry
in this small dying place
whose every house is now lived in
by the sad widow of a fine strong man.

There were fine strong men in the Duke's time.
He drove them to the shore, he drove them
to Canada. He gave no friendly thought to them
as he turned his coach and four
on the sweet green sward
by the Place for Pulling up Boats
where no boats are.

A man in Assynt

Glaciers, grinding West, gouged out
these valleys, rasping the brown sandstone,
and left, on the hard rock below – the
ruffled foreland –
this frieze of mountains, filed
on the blue air – Stac Polly,
Cul Beag, Cul Mor, Suilven,
Canisp – a frieze and
a litany.

Who owns this landscape?
Has owning anything to do with love?
For it and I have a love-affair, so nearly human
we even have quarrels. –
When I intrude too confidently
it rebuffs me with a wind like a hand
or puts in my way
a quaking bog or a loch
where no loch should be. Or I turn stonily
away, refusing to notice
the rouged rocks, the mascara
under a dripping ledge, even
the tossed, the stony limbs waiting.

I can't pretend
it gets sick for me in my absence,
though I get
sick for it. Yet I love it
with special gratitude, since
it sends me no letters, is never
jealous and, expecting nothing
from me, gets nothing but
cigarette packets and footprints.

Who owns this landscape? –
The millionaire who bought it or
the poacher staggering downhill in the early morning
with a deer on his back?

Who possesses this landscape? –
The man who bought it or
I who am possessed by it?

False questions, for
this landscape is
masterless
and intractable in any terms
that are human.
It is docile only to the weather
and its indefatigable lieutenants –

wind, water and frost.
The wind whets the high ridges
and stunts silver birches and alders.
Rain falling down meets
springs gushing up –
they gather and carry down to the Minch
tons of sour soil, making bald
the bony scalp of Cul Mor. And frost
thrusts his hand in cracks and, clenching his fist,
bursts open the sandstone plates,
the armour of Suilven;
he bleeds stories down chutes and screes,
smelling of gunpowder.

Or has it come to this,
that this dying landscape belongs
to the dead, the crofters and fighters
and fishermen whose larochs
sink into the bracken
by Loch Assynt and Loch Crocach? –
to men trampled under the hoofs of sheep
and driven by deer to
the ends of the earth – to men whose loyalty
was so great it accepted their own betrayal
by their own chiefs and whose descendants now
are kept in their place
by English businessmen and the indifference
of a remote and ignorant government.

Where have they gone, the people
who lived between here and
Quinag, that tall
huddle of anvils that puffs out
two ravens into the blue and
looks down on the lochs of Stoer
where trout idle among reeds and
waterlilies – take one of them home
and smell, in a flower
the sepulchral smell of water.

Beyond Fewin lies the Veyatie Burn – fine
crossing place for deer, they trot over
with frills of water flouncing
at their knees. That water rests in Fewin
beneath the sandstone hulk
of Suilven, not knowing what's to come –
the clattering horserush down
the Kirkaig gorge, the sixty-foot
Falls ... There are twenty-one pools
on the Kirkaig ... Since
before empires were possible
till now, when so many have died
in their own dust,
the Kirkaig Falls have been walking backwards –
twenty-one paces up their own stream.
Salmon lie
in each of the huge footprints.
You can try to catch them –
at a price.
The man whose generations of ancestors
fished this, their own river,
can catch them still –
at a price ...

The salmon come from the sea. I watch
its waves thumping down their glossy arches in
a soup of sand, folding over from one
end of the bay to the other.
Sandpipers, ringed plover, turnstones
play tig with these waves that
pay no heed but laboriously get on with
playing their million-finger exercises on
the keyboard of the sand.

The salmon come from the sea. Men
go out on it. The *Valhalla*, the *Golden Emblem*
come in, smoking with gulls,
from the fishing grounds of the Minch
to lie, docile, by the Culag pier.

Beneath it the joppling water
shuffles its blues and greens till they almost
waver the burly baulks away.
From the tall bows ropes reach ashore
in languid arcs, till, through rings, round
bollards, they clot and
twist themselves in savage knots.
The boats lie still with a cargo
of fish and voyages.

Hard labour can relax.
The salty smell outside, which is made up
of brine and seaweed
and fish, reaches the pub door but
is refused admittance. Here,
men in huge jerseys drink small drinks.
The thick talk
of fishing and sheep is livened
by a witty crackle of gossip
and the bitter last tale
of local politics. At ten o'clock, the barman
will stop whistling a strathspey to shout
'Time, please!' and they
will noisily trail out, injecting a guff of alcohol
into the salty smell made up
of brine and seaweed
and fish, which stretches from the pub door
all the way to America.

Whom does the sea belong to?
Fat governments? Guillemots? Or men
who steal from it what they can
to support their dying acres?

Fish from the sea, for Glasgow, London,
Edinburgh. But the land, too, sells
itself; and from these places
come people tired of a new civilisation
to taste what's left

of an old one. They outnumber
the locals – a thing
too easy to do … In Lochinver,
Achmelvich, Clashnessie, Clachtoll
they exchange the tyranny of the clock
for the natural rhythm of day and
night and day and night and for
the natural decorum that binds together
the fishing grounds, crofting lands
and the rough sheepruns that hoist themselves
towards the hills. They meet the people
and are not rejected. In the sweating night
London and Edinburgh fall away
under the bouncing rhythms of *Strip the Willow*
and the *Gay Gordons*, and when the lights go out
and all the goodnights are spoken, they can hear
a drunk melodeon go without staggering
along the dark road.

But the night's not over. A twinkle of light
in Strathan, Brackloch, Inveruplan, shows
where the tales are going round, tall
as the mast of the *Valhalla*, and songs are sung
by keeper, shepherd and fisherman,
each tilting his Rembrandt face in the light
and banging the chorus round, till, with a shout
he takes up his dram and drinks it down.
The Gauger of Dalmore lives again
in verses. An old song
makes history alive again,
as a rickle of stones peoples the dark theatre
of the mind with a shouting crowd and,
in the middle, MacLeod of Assynt and
his greater prisoner – Montrose.

An old song. A rickle of stones. A
name on a map.
I read on a map a name whose Gaelic means
the Battlefield of the Big Men.

I think of yelling hosts, banners,
counterattacks, deployments. When I get there,
it's ten acres, ten small acres
of boggy ground.
I feel
I am looking through the same wrong end
of the same telescope
through which I look back through time
and see
Christ, Socrates, Dante – all the Big Men
picked out, on their few acres,
clear and tiny in
the misty landscape of history.

Up from that mist crowds
the present. This day has lain long,
has dozed late, till
the church bell jerks and, wagging madly
in its salty tower, sends its voice
clanking through the sabbath drowse.
And dark minds in black clothes gather like
bees to the hive, to share
the bitter honey of the Word, to submit
to the hard judgment of a God
my childhood God would have a difficulty
in recognising.
Ten yards from the sea's surge
they sing to Him beautiful praises
that surge like the sea,
in a bare stone box built
for the worship of the Creator
of all colours and between-colours, and of
all shapes, and of the holiness
of identity and of the purifying light-stream
of reason. The sound of that praise
escapes from the stone box
and takes its place in the ordinary communion
of all sounds, that are
Being expressing itself – as it does in its continuous,

its never-ending creation of leaves,
birds, waves, stone boxes – and beliefs,
the true and the false.

These shapes; these incarnations, have their own determined
identities, their own dark holiness, their
high absurdities. See how they make
a breadth and assemblage of animals,
a perpendicularity of creatures, from where,
three thousand feet up, two ravens go by
in their seedy, nonchalant way, down to
the burn-mouth where baby mussels
drink fresh water through their beards –
or down, down still, to where the masked conger eel
goes like a gangster through
the weedy slums at the sea's foot.

Greenshank, adder, wildcat, guillemot, seatrout,
fox and falcon – the list winds through
all the crooks and crannies of this landscape, all
the subtleties and shifts of its waters and
the prevarications of its air –
while roofs fall in, walls crumble, gables
die last of all, and man becomes,
in this most beautiful corner of the land,
one of the rare animals.

Up there, the scraping light
whittles the cloud edges till, like thin bone,
they're bright with their own opaque selves. Down here,
a skinny rosebush is an eccentric jug
of air. They make me,
somewhere between them,
a visiting eye,
an unrequited passion,
watching the tide glittering backward and making
its huge withdrawal from beaches
and kilted rocks. And the mind
behind the eye, within the passion,

remembers with certainty that the tide will return
and thinks, with hope, that that other ebb,
that sad withdrawal of people, may, too,
reverse itself and flood
the bays and the sheltered glens
with new generations replenishing the land
with its richest of riches and coming, at last,
into their own again.

Old Edinburgh

Down the Canongate
down the Cowgate
go vermilion dreams
snake's tongues of bannerets
trumpets with words from their mouths
saying *Praise me, praise me.*

Up the Cowgate
up the Canongate
lice on the march
tar on the amputated stump
Hell speaking with the tongue of Heaven
a woman tied to the tail of a cart.

And history leans by a dark entry
with words from his mouth
that say *Pity me, pity me*
but never forgive.

Battlefield near Inverness

Only dead bodies lie here,
for dreams are not to be buried.
You can't keep down with a stone
the stink of loyalty and honour
that still poison the air
with all the corpses they've made
since the air rotted at Culloden.

Rewards and furies

In a ship hardly bigger than this room,
with a mind narrower than this pen,
with a library of one book
and that book with one word in it,
Columbus sailed and sailed and arrived.

The poor soul didn't know where.
Still, he succeeded:
Indians were massacred, railways
opened up wheatfields, jails and asylums,
and skyscrapers walked around
with atom bombs slung at their hips.

I hope Columbus didn't believe
in his own ghost. How could it rest
through these hundreds of years?
How could it stare into the future
at his monstrous descendants
ignorantly sailing, ignorantly arriving?

Queen of Scots

Mary was depressed.
She hadn't combed her red hair yet.
She hadn't touched her frightful Scottish breakfast.
Her lady-in-waiting, another Mary,
had told Rizzio Her Majesty wasn't at home,
a lie so obvious it was another way
of telling the truth.

Mary was depressed.
She wanted real life and here she was
acting in a real play, with real blood in it.

And she thought of the years to come
and of the frightful plays that would be written
about the play she was in.

She said something in French
and with her royal foot she kicked
the spaniel that was gazing at her
with exophthalmic adoration.

At the Loch of the Pass of the Swans

I dangle my feet in the cool loch water.
A thousand journeys, a century of miles
crinkle to the crimson flower beside me.

Where is the mist that wrapped itself round
the threshing machine last autumn?
Where's the blackface lamb I pulled from a peat bog?

Where are the places my father knew
and the storm waves roaring in the caves of Scarp,
frightening my little girl mother?

Escape from my history – to the campfires
of Huns and Goths, to the monks picking
hazel nuts and berries on sunny Iona.

I play with time and distance,
a game less cruel than the one
they play with me, the one they will win.

Let them. For this moment they've shrunk
to the crimson flower beside me
and two feet, corpse-white, in the smiling water.

Characteristics

My American friends,
who claim Scottish ancestry,
have been touring Scotland.
In ten days they visited
eleven castles. I smiled –
How American.
They said they preferred
the ruined ones. I smiled again.
How Scottish.

From My Window

From my window

Outside, there are gardens full of trees
that have not yet fruited and a silence
waiting to grow apples of music
and clustering berries of words.

If I could sweep away those clouds
a moon would stare at me,
uncomprehending, meaningless and lonely.

A truck goes by. In the noise it makes
there's a mutilated shape
struggling to become
a cousin of Beethoven, a sweet child
of Mozart.

A group of teenagers turns the corner.
Raucous voices. Dyed hair.
Tribal badges.

I stare down at them, like the moon,
uncomprehending, meaningless and lonely.

What visions are waiting to be born
in their sad eyes?
What loving gesture weeps for itself
in the ugly angles of their arms?

November night, Edinburgh

The night tinkles like ice in glasses.
Leaves are glued to the pavement with frost.
The brown air fumes at the shop windows,
Tries the doors, and sidles past.

I gulp down winter raw. The heady
Darkness swirls with tenements.
In a brown fuzz of cottonwool
Lamps fade up crags, die into pits.

Frost in my lungs is harsh as leaves
Scraped up on paths. – I look up, there,
A high roof sails, at the mast-head
Fluttering a grey and ragged star.

The world's a bear shrugged in his den.
It's snug and close in the snoring night.
And outside like chrysanthemums
The fog unfolds its bitter scent.

Edinburgh courtyard in July

Hot light is smeared as thick as paint
On these ramshackle tenements. Stones smell
Of dust. Their hoisting into quaint
Crowsteps, corbels, carved with fool and saint,
Holds fathoms of heat, like water in a well.

Cliff-dwellers have poked out from their
High cave-mouths brilliant rags on drying-lines;
They hang still, dazzling in the glare,
And lead the eye up, ledge by ledge, to where
A chimney's tilted helmet winks and shines.

And water from a broken drain
Splashes a glassy hand out in the air
That breaks in an unbraiding rain
And falls still fraying, to become a stain
That spreads by footsteps, ghosting everywhere.

Hotel room, 12th floor

This morning I watched from here
a helicopter skirting like a damaged insect
the Empire State Building, that
jumbo size dentist's drill, and landing

on the roof of the PanAm skyscraper.
But now midnight has come in
from foreign places. Its uncivilised darkness
is shot at by a million lit windows, all
ups and acrosses

But midnight is not
so easily defeated. I lie in bed, between
a radio and a television set, and hear
the wildest of warwhoops continually ululating through
the glittering canyons and gulches –
police cars and ambulances racing
to the broken bones, the harsh screaming
from coldwater flats, the blood
glazed on sidewalks.

The frontier is never
somewhere else. And no stockades
can keep the midnight out.

Last night in New York

A fortnight is long enough
to live on a roller-coaster.
Princes Street, Edinburgh, even in the most rushed
of rush hours, you'll be
a glade in a wood, I'll
foretell the weather, I'll be
a hick in the sticks.

The sun goes up on Edinburgh.
Manhattan goes up on the sun.
Her buildings overtop Arthur's Seat
and are out of date as soon as
a newspaper. Last year's artist is
a caveman. Tomorrow's best seller
has still to be born.

I plunge through constellations
and basements. My brain spins up there,
I pass it on its way down. I can't see
for the skyscraper in my eye, there's a traffic jam
in my ears. My hands are tacky
with steering my bolting self
through unlikelihoods and impossibilities.
Flags and circuses orbit
my head, I am haloed but not saintly –
poor Faust in 42nd Street.
The tugs in the East River butt
rafts of freight trucks through
my veins. I look at my watch
and its face is Times Square
glittering and crawling with invitations.

Two weeks on a roller-coaster
is long enough. I remember
all islands are not called Coney.
I think, Tomorrow my head will be
higher than my feet, my brain
will come home, I'll be able
to catch up on myself – and, tilting my halo,
I walk out into
exploding precincts and street-bursts.

Antique shop window

Spearsman of molasses, shepherdess
cut from a sugarblock, rings with
varicose stones – all
on a one-legged table perched
on a birdclaw.

And your face in the glass and
my face in the glass, and the real world
behind us translated before us

into dim images, there
– so that the spearsman crouches
on a bird-legged table in
a busy street and the shepherdess runs
through head after head after head
and who can tell
if your face is haunted by the world
or the world by your face?

Look left at the birds stitched
still in their singing, at the sword
half drawn from the scabbard – look left,
more left, to me, this side of the window,
a two-legged, man-legged cabinet
of antique feelings, all of them
genuine.

Milne's Bar

Cigarette smoke floated
in an Eastern way
a yard above the slopped tables.

The solid man thought
nothing could hurt him
as long as he didn't show it –

a stoicism of a kind. I
was inclined to agree with him,
having had a classical education.

To prove it, he went on telling
of terrible things that had
happened to him –

so boringly, my mind
skipped away among the glasses
and floated, in an Eastern way,

a yard above the slopped
table; when it looked down,
the solid man

was crying into his own mouth.
I caught sight of myself
in a mirror

and stared, rather admiring
the look of suffering
in my middle-aged eyes.

Gone are the days

Impossible to call a lamb a lambkin
or say eftsoons or spell you ladye.
My shining armour bleeds when it's scratched;
I blow the nose that's part of my visor.

When I go pricking o'er the plain
I say *Eightpence please* to the sad conductress.
The towering landscape you live in has printed
on its portcullis *Bed and breakfast*.

I don't regret it. There are wildernesses
enough in Rose Street or the Grassmarket
where dragons' breaths are methylated
and social workers trap the unwary.

So don't expect me, lady with no e,
to look at a lamb and feel lambkin
or give me a down look because I bought
my greaves and cuisses at Marks and Spencers.

Pishtushery's out. But oh, how my heart swells
to see you perched, perjink, on a bar stool.
And though epics are shrunk to epigrams, let me
buy a love potion, a gin, a double.

Neighbour

His car sits outside the house.
It never goes anywhere. Is it
a pet?

When he goes for his morning paper
he makes a perfect right-angle
at the corner.

What does he do at home? Sit at attention?
Or does he stay in the lobby
like a hatstand?

Does his wife know she married
a diagram? That she goes to bed
with a faded blueprint?

When I meet him
he greets me with a smile
he must have bought somewhere.

His eyes are two teaspoons
that have been emptied
for the last time.

University staff club

If a thing exists ... How I hate sentences,
Mr Professor, that begin with *if*.
Tilt your nose, Mr Professor, and sniff

The vinegar of existence with a wild rose growing in it,
Hear the ravishing harmony dunted with a drum thud.
Put a hand on your throat – that beating is blood,

Not a pussyfooting echo of remote subjunctives.
The name of a thing means one thing and
The thing means another: fanfare for the ampersand.

That joins and separates them with a third meaning.
Good ampersand: bad murderous if.
Tilt your nose, Mr Professor: there's a whiff

Of heretical impatience in your fantasies
That won't let the world be. Are you so wise
You can add one more to the world's impossibles?

Edinburgh stroll

I leave the Tollcross traffic and walk by the Meadows
between two rows of trees, all looking
as grave as Elders of the Kirk – but
wait till the wind blows.

Dogs are hunting for smells. A few men
are practising approach shots
on the dwarfish golf course. Some children
are incomprehensibly playing.

And between two heaps of jackets
a boy scores a goal –
the best one ever,

Past the Infirmary I go back to the traffic,
cross it, and there's Sandy Bell's Bar.

Tollcross to Sandy Bell's Bar –
a short walk with a long conclusion.

Five minutes at the window

A boy, in loops and straights, skateboards
down the street. In number 20
a tree with lights for flowers
says it's Christmas.

The pear tree across the road shivers
in a maidenly breeze. I know
Blackford Pond will be
a candelabra of light.

A seagull tries over and over again
to pick up something on the road.
Oh, the motorcars.
And a white cat sits halfway up a tree.
Why?

Trivia. What are trivia?
They've blown away my black mood.
I smile at the glass of freesias on the table.
My shelves of books say nothing
but I know what they mean.
I'm back in the world again
and am happy in spite of
its disasters, its horrors, its griefs.

Foggy night

We put the tea things on the table
and turn on the TV for the News.
I look at the brown teapot, almost expecting it
to cluck.

Night is heavy on the city.
The lights struggle and on the Firth of Forth
a foghorn is suffering.

But space, good space, does not desert us.
In it the clock's voice plods on the mantelpiece
and a petal falls on the table.

The line of its fall is a fence
between the millions of years that have gone
and the millions to come.

Balances

Balances

Because I see the world poisoned
by cant and brutal self-seeking,
must I be silent about
the useless waterlily, the dunnock's nest
in the hedgeback?

Because I am fifty-six years old
must I love, if I love at all,
only ideas – not people, but only
the idea of people?

Because there is work to do, to steady
a world jarred off balance,
must a man meet only a fellow-worker
and never a man?

There are more meanings than those
in text books of economics
and a part of the worst slum
is the moon rising over it
and eyes weeping and
mouths laughing.

Equilibrist

I see an adder and, a yard away,
a butterfly being gorgeous. I switch the radio
from tortures in foreign prisons
to a sonata of Schubert (that foreigner).
I crawl from the swamp of nightmare into
a glittering rainfall, a swathing of sunlight.

Noticing you can do nothing about.
It's the balancing that shakes my mind.

What my friends don't notice
is the weight of joy in my right hand
and the weight of sadness in my left.
All they see is MacCaig being upright,
easy-oasy and jocose.

I had a difficulty in being friendly
to the Lord, who gave us these burdens,
so I returned him to other people
and totter without help
among his careless inventions.

Spate in winter midnight

The streams fall down and through the darkness bear
Such wild and shaking hair,
Such looks beyond a cool surmise,
Such lamentable uproar from night skies
As turn the owl from honey of blood and make
Great stags stand still to hear the darkness shake.

Through Troys of bracken and Babel towers of rocks
Shrinks now the looting fox,
Fearful to touch the thudding ground
And flattened to it by the mastering sound.
And roebuck stilt and leap sideways; their skin
Twitches like water on the fear within.

Black hills are slashed white with this falling grace
Whose violence buckles space
To a sheet-iron thunder. This
Is noise made universe, whose still centre is
Where the cold adder sleeps in his small bed,
Curled neatly round his neat and evil head.

July evening

A bird's voice chinks and tinkles
Alone in the gaunt reedbed –
   Tiny silversmith
Working late in the evening.

I sit and listen. The rooftop
With a quill of smoke stuck in it
   Wavers against the sky
In the dreamy heat of summer.

Flowers' closing time: bee lurches
Across the hayfield, singing
   And feeling its drunken way
Round the air's invisible corners.

And grass is grace. And charlock
Is gold of its own bounty.
   The broken chair by the wall
Is one with immortal landscapes.

Something has been completed
That everything is part of,
   Something that will go on
Being completed forever.

Visiting hour

The hospital smell
combs my nostrils
as they go bobbing along
green and yellow corridors.

What seems a corpse
is trundled into a lift and vanishes
heavenward.

I will not feel, I will not
feel, until
I have to.

Nurses walk lightly, swiftly,
here and up and down and there,
their slender waists miraculously
carrying their burden
of so much pain, so
many deaths, their eyes
still clear after
so many farewells.

Ward 7. She lies
in a white cave of forgetfulness.
A withered hand
trembles on its stalk. Eyes move
behind eyelids too heavy
to raise. Into an arm wasted
of colour a glass fang is fixed,
not guzzling but giving.
And between her and me
distance shrinks till there is none left
but the distance of pain that neither she nor I
can cross.

She smiles a little at this
black figure in her white cave
who clumsily rises
in the round swimming waves of a bell
and dizzily goes off, growing fainter,
not smaller, leaving behind only
books that will not be read
and fruitless fruits.

Assisi

The dwarf with his hands on backwards
sat, slumped like a half-filled sack
on tiny twisted legs from which
sawdust might run,
outside the three tiers of churches built
in honour of St Francis, brother
of the poor, talker with birds, over whom
he had the advantage
of not being dead yet.

A priest explained
how clever it was of Giotto
to make his frescoes tell stories
that would reveal to the illiterate the goodness
of God and the suffering
of His Son. I understood
the explanation and
the cleverness.

A rush of tourists, clucking contentedly,
fluttered after him as he scattered
the grain of the Word. It was they who had passed
the ruined temple outside, whose eyes
wept pus, whose back was higher
than his head, whose lopsided mouth
said *Grazie* in a voice as sweet
as a child's when she speaks to her mother
or a bird's when it spoke
to St Francis.

Smuggler

Watch him when he opens
his bulging words – justice,
fraternity, freedom, internationalism, peace,
peace, peace. Make it your custom
to pay no heed
to his frank look, his visas, his stamps
and signatures. Make it
your duty to spread out their contents
in a clear light.

Nobody with such luggage
has nothing to declare.

Interruption to a journey

The hare we had run over
bounced about the road
on the springing curve
of its spine.

Cornfields breathed in the darkness.
We were going through the darkness and
the breathing cornfields from one
important place to another.

We broke the hare's neck
and made that place, for a moment,
the most important place there was,
where a bowstring was cut
and a bow broken for ever
that had shot itself through so many
darknesses and cornfields.

It was left in that landscape.
It left us in another.

Vestey's well

We raised the lid. The cold spring water was
So clear it wasn't there.
At the foot of its non-depth a grave toad squatted
As still as Buddha in his non-place. Flaws
Breathed on the water – he trembled to no-where
Then steadied into being again. A fretted
Fern was his Bo-tree. Time in that delicate place
Sat still for ever staring in its own face.

We filled the jam-jar with bright nothing and
Drank down its freezing light
That the sun burned us with (that raging planet
That will not stand and will not understand)
And tried to feel we were each one a bright
And delicate place with a philosopher in it –
And failed; and let the hinged lid slowly fall.
The little Buddha hadn't moved at all.

Notations of ten summer minutes

A boy skips flat stones out to sea – each does fine
till a small wave meets it head on and swallows it.
The boy will do the same.

The schoolmaster stands looking out of the window
with one Latin eye and one Greek one.
A boat rounds the point in Gaelic.

Out of the shop comes a stream
of Omo, Weetabix, BiSoDol tablets and a man
with a pocket shaped like a whisky bottle.

Lord V. walks by with the village in his pocket.
Angus walks by
spending the village into the air.

A melodeon is wheezing a clear-throated jig
on the deck of the *Arcadia*. On the shore hills Pan
cocks a hairy ear; and falls asleep again.

The ten minutes are up, except they aren't.
I leave the village, except I don't.
The jig fades to silence, except it doesn't.

Intruder in a set scene

The way the water goes is blink blink blink.
That heap of trash was once
a swan's throne. The swans now lean their chests
against the waves that spill on Benbecula.
On the towpath a little girl
peers over the handle of the pram she's pushing.
Her mother follows her, reading a letter.

Everything is winter, everything
is a letter from another place, measuring
absence. Everything laments
the swan, drifting and dazzling on a western sealoch.

– But the little girl, five years of self-importance,
walks in her own season, not noticing
the stop-go's of water, the mouldering swan-throne,
the tears turning cold in the eyes of her mother.

Adrift

More like a raft than a boat
the world I sail on.

I say I'm not troubled – I accept
the powerful hospitality of the tides.

But I write little communications and float them off
to anywhere.

Some are Ophelias witless and singing
among the foam flowers.
But others are Orpheus lamenting
a harbour, a house there, and a girl in it.

Sea change

I think of Lycidas drowned
in Milton's mind.
How elegantly he died. How languorously
he moved
in those baroque currents. No doubt
sea nymphs wavered round him
in melodious welcome.

And I think of Roddy drowned
off Cape Wrath, gulping
fistfuls of salt, eyes bursting, limbs thrashing
the ponderous green. – No elegance here,
nor in the silent welcome
of conger and dogfish and crab.

Two skulls

MacDiarmid found a pigeon's skull
on the bright shore turf of a Hebridean island.

I found the skull of a dogfish
on the sand at Cleethorpes.

His: the skull of a twirler and staller,
a rocketer, a headlong grace, symbol of peace.

Mine: hooverer of the sea's floor, sneak thief
of herrings from nets, corpse-eater, emblem of nightmare.

After death the one is as beautiful as the other
(but not to a pigeon, not to a dogfish).

I hate death, the skull-maker, because he proves
that destroying and making happen together.

He'll be no friend of mine, as long as I'm still
a feathery pigeon or a scrapeskin dogfish.

– I mean a man, whose skull contains
ideas death never thought of.

They'll cheat him, for they'll lodge in another skull
–   or become nothing, that comfortable absolute.

So many summers

Beside one loch, a hind's neat skeleton,
Beside another, a boat pulled high and dry:
Two neat geometries drawn in the weather:
Two things already dead and still to die.

I passed them every summer, rod in hand,
Skirting the bright blue or the spitting gray,
And, every summer, saw how the bleached timbers
Gaped wider and the neat ribs fell away.

Time adds one malice to another one –
Now you'd look very close before you knew
If it's the boat that ran, the hind went sailing.
So many summers, and I have lived them too.

Sounds of the day

When a clatter came,
it was horses crossing the ford.
When the air creaked, it was
a lapwing seeing us off the premises
of its private marsh. A snuffling puff
ten yards from the boat was the tide blocking and
unblocking a hole in a rock.
When the black drums rolled, it was water
falling sixty feet into itself.

When the door
scraped shut, it was the end
of all the sounds there are.

You left me
beside the quietest fire in the world.

I thought I was hurt in my pride only,
forgetting that,
when you plunge your hand in freezing water,
you feel
a bangle of ice round your wrist

before the whole hand goes numb.

Small boy

He picked up a pebble
and threw it into the sea.

And another, and another.
He couldn't stop.

He wasn't trying to fill the sea.
He wasn't trying to empty the beach.

He was just throwing away,
nothing else but.

Like a kitten playing
he was practising for the future

when there'll be so many things
he'll want to throw away

if only his fingers will unclench
and let them go.

Old poet

The alder tree
shrivelled by the salt wind
has lived so long
it has carried and sheltered
its own weight
of nests.

In That Other World

In that other world

They sit at their long table
in a room so long it's a tunnel,
in a tunnel with a green roof
on which sometimes a flower nods
as if to remind them of something.

They talk about everything
except Death, but they don't listen
to each other. They talk, staring
straight in front of them.
And they tremble.

The only time they notice each other
is when Death sweeps past them
with his keys clinking and a long pen
in his hand.

Then they look shyly at each other
for a moment before staring ahead
and talking, talking, trying to remember
what a flower is,
trying to remember
why they are here.

Loch Sionascaig

Hard to remember how the water went
Shaking the light,
Until it shook like peas in a riddling plate.

Or how the islands snored into the wind,
Or seemed to, round
Stiff, plunging headlands that they never cleared.

Or how a trout hung high its drizzling bow
For a count of three –
Heraldic figure on a shield of spray.

Yet clear the footprint in the puddled sand
That slowly filled
And rounded out and smoothed and disappeared.

Descent from the Green Corrie

The climb's all right, it's the descent that kills you.
Knees become fists that don't know how to clench
And thighs are strings in parallel.
Gravity's still your enemy; it drills you
With your own backbone – its love is all to wrench
You down on screes or boggy asphodel

And the elation that for a moment fills you
Beside the misty cairn's that lesser thing
A memory of it. It's not
The punishing climb, it's the descent that kills you
However sweetly the valley thrushes sing
And shadows darken with the peace they've brought.

Memorial

Everywhere she dies. Everywhere I go she dies.
No sunrise, no city square, no lurking beautiful mountain
but has her death in it.
The silence of her dying sounds through
the carousel of language, it's a web
on which laughter stitches itself. How can my hand
clasp another's when between them
is that thick death, that intolerable distance?

She grieves for my grief. Dying, she tells me
that bird dives from the sun, that fish
leaps into it. No crocus is carved more gently
than the way her dying
shapes my mind. – But I hear, too,

the other words,
black words that make the sound
of soundlessness, that name the nowhere
she is continuously going into.

Ever since she died
she can't stop dying. She makes me
her elegy. I am a walking masterpiece,
a true fiction
of the ugliness of death.
I am her sad music.

Old man thinking

Oars, held still, drop
on black water
tiny roulades
of waterdrops.
With their little sprinkling
they people
a big silence.

You who are long gone,
my thoughts of you are like that:
a delicate, clear population
in the big silence
where I rest on the oars and
my boat
hushes ashore.

Poems for Angus

Notes on a winter journey, and a footnote

1

The snow's almost faultless. It bounces back
the sun's light but can do nothing with
those two stags, their cold noses, their yellow teeth.

2

On the loch's eye a cataract is forming.
Fistfuls of white make the telephone wires
loop after loop of snow buntings.

3

So few cars, they leave the snow snow.
I think of the horrible marzipan
in the streets of Edinburgh.

4

The hotel at Ullapool, that should be a bang of light,
is crepuscular. The bar is fireflied
with whisky glasses.

5

At Inchnadamph snow is falling. The windscreen wipers
squeak and I stare through
a segment of a circle. What more do I ever do? ...

6

(Seventeen miles to go. I didn't know it, but when
I got there a death waited for me – that segment
shut its fan: and a blinding winter closed in.)

A. K. MacLeod

I went to the landscape I love best
and the man who was its meaning and added to it
met me at Ullapool.

The beautiful landscape was under snow
and was beautiful in a new way.

Next morning, the man who had greeted me
with the pleasure of pleasure
vomited blood
and died.

Crofters and fishermen and womenfolk, unable
to say any more, said,
'It's a grand day, it's a beautiful day.'

And I thought, 'Yes, it is.'
And I thought of him lying there,
the dead centre of it all.

Praise of a man

He went through a company like a lamplighter –
see the dull minds, one after another,
begin to glow, to shed
a benificent light.

He went through a company like
a knifegrinder – see the dull minds
scattering sparks of themselves,
becoming razory, becoming useful.

He went through a company
as himself. But now he's one
of the multitudinous company of the dead
where are no individuals.

The benificent lights dim
but don't vanish. The razory edges
dull but still cut. He's gone: but you can see
his tracks still, in the snow of the world.

Angus's dog

Black collie, do you remember yourself?

Do you remember your name was Mephistopheles,
though (as if you were only a little devil)
everyone called you Meph?

You'd chase everything – sea gulls, motor cars,
jet planes. (It's said you once set off
after a lightning flash.) Half over a rock,
you followed the salmon fly arcing
through the bronze water. You loved everything
except rabbits – though
you grinned away under the bed
when your master came home
drink taken. How you'd lay your head
on a visitor's knee and look up, so soulfully,
like George Eliot playing Sarah Bernhardt.

… Black Meph, how can you remember yourself
in that blank no-time, no-place where
you can't even greet your master
though he's there too?

In memoriam

On that stormy night
a top branch broke off
on the biggest tree in my garden.

It's still up there. Though its leaves
are withered black among the green
the living branches
won't let it fall.

Her illness

For this once I force myself
to write down the word *light*.
So many times in the last cloudy months
I've tried to and my mouth
said *dark*.

For the waters of Babylon
sound in my friendly river, my harp
hangs in a familiar tree.

I used not to care
that there never were unicorns
and that a phoenix was only
a metaphor on fire.
I knew that, but I loved them.

But truth has been stripped of its flesh,
its eyes, its gentle hands.
It reaches out an arm and lays
five cold bones on my knee.
It never stops smiling
with a changed smile.

Myself after her death

1

I'm exiled from what used to be
my country. It welcomed me
with gifts of peace and of storms,
with heights of mountains
and altitudes of joy.

Not now.
No, says the wall, and I turn back.
No, says the mountain
and I sit sad in the valley
listening to the river that says
Trespasser, trespasser, trespasser.

I stubbornly say, All the same
it's still beautiful.
And I know that's true
but I know also
why it fails to recognise me.

Myself after her death

2

That boulder beside Loch na Barrack,
stuck all over with tiny pebbles,
its costume jewellery
– that's what I'm like.

I have a hardness in me too
of a human kind and –
look close and you'll see
the costume jewellery I've stolen
from the past,
more precious to me
than opals and diamonds
and emeralds.

Myself after her death

When she was alive
I had no need for hope,
When she was dying
hope never visited us.

In this cold city snow is falling.
But life works underground and over it
at the endless toil of creation.
Little comfort for me.

But I have blessings; I count them.
They have the names of people.
There are others. But above all
they have the names of people.

They will die, as she did.
They will die, as I will.
And I look at the face of death
and say, I hate you, to destroy such wonders.

Found guilty

To this day, poor swimmer as I am,
it grieves me
that I watched the little sandpiper drown.

When I passed the nest
shoulder high on a bank of Loch Lurgain
the young ones cheeped-cheeped out of it
to flop in the heather twenty yards away.

Except that one. It flew over the water,
lower and lower, then tried to fly in the water:
and drowned.

I've watched friends, strong fliers among mountains,
who flew lower and lower
and drowned in the uncaring water
they had soared above.

Little sandpiper, you left me
accused of what
I have no defence against.

Friends, I ask your forgiveness.
I ask for something
I don't deserve. And I ask for it
too late.

A Man in My Position

A man in my position

Hear my words carefully.
Some are spoken
not by me, but
by a man in my position.

What right has he
to use my mouth? I hate him
when he touches you
the wrong way.

Yet he loves you also,
this appalling stranger
who makes windows of my eyes.
You see him looking out.

Until he dies
of my love for you
hear my words carefully –
for who is talking now?

Party

Watching your face
That makes an emptiness of this crowded place,
I stand, not speaking, terrified to see
You grown more lovely, and still lost to me.

Estuary

Saltings and eelgrass
and mud dimpling under the moon –
a place for curlews but not for me; a place
for dunlin, godwit, sandpiper, turnstone
but not for me.

The light is blue. The far away tide
shines like a fish in a cupboard.

I see the blues of your eyes.

Don't step on the little green crab.
Don't step on the mud hump, it will hold you
in a soft fist.

Your brow shines. The inside
of a mussel shell shines. I make
horrible correspondences.

Somewhere behind us
a clear river has died, its muscles
gone slack, its innumerable voices turned
into sounds of sucking and slithering.

Can we turn back? Let me take
your hand, cold as eelgrass, and look for
a meadow trimmed with fresh water, let me
turn the blues of your eyes away
from the moon dimpling in mud.

By correspondence then
your eyes will be clear, you will
sometimes look at me, you will laugh
at the lolloping hare or the hedgehog trundling by
like a mediaeval siege engine – at a world
of beginnings, at a world of possibly
desperate ends, but
a world of beginnings.

Song without music

I saw a hind (with time enough to stare).
I saw a trout flip up into the air.
I saw a flower whose name I wished I knew –
Outlined in white and shaded in with blue.

I heard a water sliding over stones.
I heard your voice in its sweet overtones.
I heard your voice, but saw you not at all,
Not even as ghost in the white waterfall.

Names

In that shallow water
swim extraordinary little fish
with extraordinary names
they don't know they've been given –
rock goby, lumpsucker, father lasher.

I sit among sea lavender and see it. Easy
to point and say buckthorn,
tamarisk, purple rocket.
But they no more know these names
than I know who named them.

I know your name and who named you.
But you have selves as secret from me
as blenny or butterfish.
I sit by you and see you
with eyes ignorant as a glasswort
and I name you and name you
and wonder how it is
that the weight of your name, the most ponderable
thing I know, should raise up
my thoughts
from one shallow pool to
another where
we move always sideways to each other, like
a velever fiddler and a porcelain crab.

Incident

I look across the table and think
(fiery with love)
Ask me, go on, ask me
to do something impossible,
something freakishly useless,
something unimaginable and inimitable
like making a finger break into blossom
or walking for half an hour in twenty minutes
or remembering tomorrow.

I will you to ask it.
But all you say is
Will you give me a cigarette, please?
And I smile and,
returning to the marvellous world
of possibility,
I give you one
with a hand that trembles
with a human trembling.

Perfect evening, Loch Roe

I pull the boat along gently. In the stern
Donald tucks his long rod under his arm
and lights his pipe.

Behind my right shoulder
the cliff Salpioder holds out
its anvil nose
over the sea.

The distances of other times,
the unmeasurable ones,
have withdrawn into nowhere at all.

– A sudden clamour. Oystercatchers
fly off from a gray rock –
their orange-red beaks; their wingbars flashing white.

The desires of other times too
have disappeared
behind the desires that lay beyond them.

And the dreams of other times
are huddled in their false country,
exiles returned to their homeland.

I feel something like love.
I can spare it, for the source of it all
is waiting, there, in the squat cottage.

Water tap

There was this hayfield,
You remember, pale gold
If it weren't hazed
With a million clover heads.

A rope of water
Frayed down – the bucket
Hoisted up a plate
Of flashing light.

The thin road screwed
Into hills; all ended
Journeys were somewhere,
But far, far.

You laughed, by the fence;
And everything that was
Hoisting water
Suddenly spilled over.

Index of Poem Titles

The dates ascribed to these poems are dates of composition taken from *The Poems of Norman MacCaig*, edited by Ewen McCaig.

Biographical Notes

NORMAN MacCAIG (1910–96) was born in Edinburgh. He lived there all his life, though lengthy annual visits to Assynt enriched his life and work. He attended the Royal High School, studied Classics at the University of Edinburgh and then trained as a teacher. Having spent years teaching in primary schools, he later taught Creative Writing at the University of Edinburgh, before joining the English department at the University of Stirling as a Lecturer and then as a Reader in Poetry.

MacCaig's reputation was recognised by the award of an OBE and the Queen's Gold Medal for Poetry and many other distinctions, but he is best remembered for his teaching, his public readings, his fruitful influence on younger writers and his continuing commitment to the lyric poem over a lifetime of creative work.

RODERICK WATSON is Emeritus Professor at the University of Stirling and was a friend and colleague of the poet during his Stirling years. He has published extensively on Hugh MacDiarmid, the literature of Scotland and many other Scottish writers, including an introduction to MacCaig, *The Poetry of Norman MacCaig* (1989) and a critical essay on his late work.